Gladness is Infectious

Other books by Warren Bluhm

How to Play a Blue Guitar
A Bridge at Crossroads
Refuse to be Afraid
A Scream of Consciousness
Myke Phoenix: The Complete Novelettes
The Imaginary Bomb
The Imaginary Revolution

The Roger Mifflin Collection

The Haunted Bookshop – Christopher Morley
Men in War – Andreas Latzko
Trivia – Logan Piersall Smith
The Man Who Was Thursday – G.K. Chesterton
The Demi-Gods – James Stephens

Also edited by Warren Bluhm

Resistance to Civil Government – Henry David Thoreau
Letters to the Citizens of the United States – Thomas Paine

Gladness is Infectious

A Book of Celebrations

By Warren Bluhm

WarrenBluhm.com

GLADNESS IS INFECTIOUS
© 2020 Warren Bluhm. All rights reserved.
Cover image: Willow The Best Dog There Is™

ISBN 978-0-9910107-8-3

Table of Contents

Look Up 1
A choice every sunrise 7
The day of awakening 8
For the joy 9
You have the power 10
The Best Dog There Is™ 12
In praise of old dogs 13
Nature or nurture? 15
To attend the breeze 17
Going from here to there 18
quite here in the moments 19
On waking 21
The best question in the world 22
Two ways to look at it all 24
It's all in the attitude 25
The call of the writer 26
A morning of snooty snobbery 27
Journey to Far Metaphor 29
Make your life a page-turner 30
Grant me the serenity 31
Just write anything until you write something 32
The infectiousness of gladness 34
Glad ... for words 35
Glad ... for music 36
Glad ... for life 37
Glad ... for independent thought 39
Glad ... for optimism 41
Glad ... for a favorite pen 43
Glad .. for winter solstice 45
Glad ... for the Bill of Rights 47
Glad ... for serendipity 49
Glad ... for what ifs 50
Choose gratitude 52

You say you want a resolution 53
The zen of coffee 55
Let it never be said 57
I believe ... 58
Remember to play 59
The writing station 61
Believe in yourself 64
How to overcome inertia 65
Here I sit among the detritus of human endeavor 66
Reflections while sitting in a lawn chair ... 67
The cycle and the sharing 69
A dog's life 70
Autumn sunshine and the promise of snow 72
Invocation 73
Realization 75
Further realization 76
Up through the time machine 77
A meal for the ages 78
The zen of early rising 80
The awesome explosion 81
Add to the beauty 83
The gift of the wind chimes 84
Words and music about words and music 85
Let's get to play 88
What we become 89
You can do it 90
No. really. 92
Turns out the key really is to just do it 93
A new dream all its own 95
Who am I again? (author's note) 96

Look Up

Sometimes, when you're feeling down, the most obvious thing to do escapes you: Look up.

There is so much sky there. And the Master Painter has produced so many masterpieces in every direction — sometimes I will take four pictures in six seconds and every one looks different, even though they were taken in the same moment.

We're used to paintings on canvas, so we're accustomed to viewing clouds in frames a foot or two wide — it's east to forget that real clouds are miles long and the sky goes on forever, as far as any human can determine. When they say "the sky's the limit," what they mean to say is: There is no limit.

In a world where there are infinite ways to box yourself into a corner and feel trapped by circumstances or lost or alone, the limitless sky reminds us there is no box, there are limitless possibilities, and there is no limit. And in a world of 7 billion people, and billions and billions of other creatures (hear that bird singing over there?), you are never quite alone.

The sky can be a little intimidating — like when it brings storms instead of sun and gentle clouds — and when you consider how tiny you are in the midst of all

GLADNESS IS INFECTIOUS

that infinity — but it also shows us how vast this world and this universe are in comparison to whatever you think you're facing alone.

So: Keep looking down at what ails you in your little corner of the universe — or look up and see the infinite ways to break out and live. Take a deep breath and choose. My advice: Look up. The possibilities are out there.

+ + +

I was locked in place. Nothing was coming out of the universe and into my heart to flow through my fingers and share. Oh, that's not true; I was writing but, as I said to a couple of friends, "I'm going through one of those phases where everything I write is crap."

My personal mission statement for writing is three words: Encourage, enlighten, entertain. How in the bejeebers do you do that from the depths of discouragement?

For some reason I thought of the many mornings I've walked outside and had my breath taken away by the big Wisconsin sky. If I have my phone in my pocket, I grab it, turn on the camera app, and capture the images to share later.

That's the answer, I thought: When you're down, look up. When you're knocked down, look up. It's a big

GLADNESS IS INFECTIOUS

sky, and your troubles are so little by comparison. You feel like they're bigger than you, but the universe is bigger than all of it. Somewhere in that big universe is the solution, and it's closer than you imagine.

+ + +

The audacity of hope — that phrase emerged from my subconscious as I sat and pondered what to write next after "closer than you imagine." Yes, it's the name of a political book written by a politician who was masquerading as something other than a politician — it's an effective disguise sometimes. But it's also a beautiful phrase.

To hope in the face of despair is an audacious act. How can you have hope when so much in life argues against hope? To start with, life's a bitch and then you die, literally. Yep, all of the struggle, the hard work, the staying alive and afloat in a sea that just seems to be trying to drown you — it all ends the same way. Death is inevitable, and sometimes it's hard to remember how much life there is to live.

Add to the beauty or add to the despair: Each of us has two choices — more than two, actually, infinite choices — but each of us adds something every day. Life has a basic arithmetic: We can add or we can subtract; we can multiply or we can divide. Or rather: It seems to have a basic arithmetic with those four choices, but in reality, we're always adding. If the aim is to subtract (that is, to destroy), we add our selves to that movement. If the aim is to add (that is, to build), or to multiply, we also add our selves. Each life adds to the world — when a life ends, it is a loss.

But we each have only one dying day — and we have thousands upon thousands of days to live. Concentrate on living: What do you have to add this moment, this day, with this life?

+ + +

So far I have consciously tried to state my case here without mentioning God. I think every reasonable soul has to wonder sometimes if this universe was created by a higher consciousness, a greater being, and we spend a lot of time forming an image and adopting beliefs around the nature of that higher consciousness, that greater being. It's hard to imagine infinity — it's hard to wrap our minds around the possibilities of that greater being — and when I reach the limits of my imagination, I encounter my doubts. That's when we adopt the concept of faith, denial, or somewhere in between. It's in my nature to believe in that higher consciousness, because it makes sense that in an infinite universe there has to be someone greater than us. It makes more common sense

GLADNESS IS INFECTIOUS

that a Creator made the universe than that it just appeared out of nowhere — although, then, who created the Creator? When you go back to the beginning of infinite time, what happened before it began? Such puzzles we weave when we try to conceive or understand the nature of this vast universe!

We anchor ourselves to an answer knowing we very likely will never have all the answers. We take comfort in the thought that we will understand when we reach the next level of existence, just as we gain understanding each day as we move through this level of existence. Those who insist, "This is all there is, this is it, this is your life, an emerging from nowhere into consciousness and death is the end," well, that's how they came to terms with the mystery. I can't imagine that this consciousness simply ends — I have to believe I experienced something before my birth and will experience something next — I even sense some memories of "before" hanging out on the edge of my consciousness — and that's how I've come to terms with the mystery.

+ + +

Wow. I rest my case. An hour has passed since I sat down and wrote, "Sometimes when you're feeling down, the obvious thing to do escapes you: Look up." And so I

GLADNESS IS INFECTIOUS

did. See where looking up takes your soul? I rest my case: Look up. There's so much life, there are so many possibilities, out there.

A choice every sunrise

Life goes on until it ends — and it does end. "What will I do with the time that's left?" is the central question of a life, isn't it?

Will I act in fear? Will I be kind? Will I love my neighbor as myself? Will I come and go in peace? Will I give more than I receive?

Or will I be none of these things, lashing out with snark and hate because I'm scared of what's happening to people, to the world, to me?

The choice is there, every morning — to ride the light out of darkness and live in peace, striving for harmony against the discord.

Love is there to give — Love is giving, not taking — Love is offering, not demanding — Love is a decision, not an emotion.

The day of awakening

I raise this creaky, lived-in achy body up on two buttocks and declare a celebration.

I see this sunshiney, run-through-a-field glorious day and sing.

I lift an ancient, oft-repeated, joyous song to the heavens.

Here I am, sky! Here I am, meadow! Touch my feet, soil! Touch my heart, scent of rose!

I wake from long dead slumber to taste the nectar of living here and now and alive and present.

You assassins of character, you spleen venters, you boilers of blood, you mongers of hate, I cast your pearls of venom into the cauldron and draw deep the intoxicating wine of now-hear-this-folks-the-time-has-come-to-dance-in-the-sunlight-and-make-a-joyful-noise.

Fie, death sayers. I declare life.

For the joy

Run for the joy of running because your spirit cannot be contained in a walk.

Write for the joy of writing because your spirit can't hold back the words.

Sing for the joy of singing because life has a melody and harmonies so pure and clear that it has to have music.

Speed across the page never-you-minding whether the phrase is perfect or awkward or pretty or odd, because the words have to spill out and never you mind whether they spilled out in a perfectly ordered order.

Because it's fun to write, or it better be, because you've spent your life writing and the spirit who has never had fun is a sullen spirit indeed.

Attend to crasftsmanship? Craft away, child, but not until after you've said it all raw and full and with all the joy you can't hold in your heart a minute more.

You have the power

Listen, kid. Listen, lady. Listen, old man.

You say you want to do something with this life? You're not content and you want to change things?

You say it doesn't have to be this way? You're right.

So what are you going to do about it?

It's your life. You can fix it. You have the power.

You say it's out of your control? Stop that.

You have the keys — right there, between your temples, and right there, connected to your wrists. Those belong to you, only you, and you can do anything you choose to do with your mind and your hands.

So what are you going to do?

Of course you're not sure. Everyone who ever tried something big had at least a flicker of doubt somewhere along the way; heck, they probably had big doubts from time to time — but they went for it and they kept going, and that made all the difference.

Of course you're not perfect or even very good at what you want to do. Nobody wrote "Yesterday" the first time they tried to write a song. Nobody won a Pulitzer for the first story they ever wrote. Nobody carved "David" the first time they tried to sculpt. Nobody won an Oscar for their first acting performance. You get started, you keep going, and you get better at it every time you do.

GLADNESS IS INFECTIOUS

Nobody changed the world the first time they tried. It's a big world with billions and billions of people on it. Changing it — even changing your teeny tiny corner of it — is going to take patience and time and not a little willpower.

Even changing you — the smallest unit of the collective and the entirety of you — will take patience and time and not a little willpower.

But it can be done — if you will it.

"I can't"? Who the heck told you that? Of course you can.

"Everyone is against me. Everything is against me"?

Do you know how big a word "Everyone" is?

Here's a clue: Almost everyone doesn't know who you are. Almost everyone doesn't care about you.

I'm not saying that to be mean. I'm saying that because billions and billions of people don't know you. But someday a whole lot of them might, if you go for it.

It's your life: All yours. Go live it.

GLADNESS IS INFECTIOUS

The Best Dog There Is™

She climbs up into bed first thing in the morning and presses herself into me in an insistent cocoon, moaning as I stroke her neck and licking my hand if I start to doze.

As we prepare to do her morning duty, she seeks out one of her rubber flying disks, because the ritual is not complete until she has chased the thing at least two or three times.

As Red and I absorb our morning reading, she sniffs through her toy collection. She may bring me a rubber ball to throw or roll in an unexpected direction so she can scramble after it. She may bring me a tattered towel for a tug of war. She may walk around the room with a squeak toy in her mouth, squeaking rhythmically as if singing or joining the conversation.

And once she tires of the game, she will flop on her back and invite me to rub her tummy, scratch her chest, massage her back or all of the above.

Weary from a parade of tasks that still await when I leave these four walls, I often perform my side of the game automatically and without really engaging my full attention. Every once in a while, though, Willow makes me realize she is teaching me to take a little time to play and enjoy this miraculous journey that is life.

GLADNESS IS INFECTIOUS

In praise of old dogs

If dog-years are one-seventh the length of people years, then Willow has reached 80, more or less. She walks and climbs stairs less certainly than before, as if she suffers the same aches and pains that my 60-something knees and back must contend with, and she looks and feels more fragile.

When you have an old dog, you've had a puppy and a decade or more of companionship and adventures and maybe a close call or two.

You've been awakened or otherwise startled by a random bark, and you've had an attentive witness to every bite of every meal and snack you ever tasted.

You've laid a comforting hand on an anxious shoulder through dozens of thunderstorms and neighborhood fireworks displays.

You've had a soft head and shoulders to massage to calm your soul and a nose on your knee to make you feel less alone in trying times.

You've thrown a ball 15,735,622 times and had it returned many of those times.

You've been lifted from the depths of despair by two brown eyes and a swift wag of a tail.

When you have an old dog, you have thousands of memories shared with a friend who can remind you of

GLADNESS IS INFECTIOUS

them all without words, just a nuzzle and a snuggle and a long, contented sigh.

GLADNESS IS INFECTIOUS

Nature or nurture?

I have a mantra that I tell Willow The Best Dog There Is™ almost every day.

You're the puppiest pup of all the pups who ever pupped.
You're the doggiest dog of all the dogs who ever dogged.
You're the willowiest Willow of all the Willows who ever willed.
You're the BEST — DOG — THERE — IS. Yes, you are.

And Willow is the sweetest, gentlest, most regal and dignified dog you'd like to know.

Her little sister, Dejah Thoris Princess of Mars, is something else. I'm more likely to ask, suspiciously, "What are you doing, Dejah?" or "Put it down, Dejah," or, the old standby, "Dejah, NO!"

She is a mischievous devil who sticks her nose everywhere and often can be seen prancing triumphantly around the house with a sock she has retrieved from the laundry basket, a piece of paper I left too close to the floor, or today's newspaper carelessly placed on the couch instead of the recycling bin. A month after we brought her home as a puppy seven years ago, she underwent emergency surgery after eating too many pebbles, bits of

GLADNESS IS INFECTIOUS

mulch, twigs, dead leaves and other miscellany, and she continues her nosy ways to this day.

Would Dejah change her ways if I showered her with a mantra more like Willow's? Or is Willow just a regal animal and Dejah a devil, to begin with?

I suppose there's only one way to find out ...

GLADNESS IS INFECTIOUS

To attend the breeze

The conversation outside my window begins as dawn's first light begins to creep overhead. Clearly the birds are communicating. Just as a puppy can get a general sense of its owner's message from the actions that accompany the words, we may think we understand the birds' language, but not the words – if words they are.

Is there a place left on Earth where the birds can speak without the drone or whine of a manmade motor in the distance? From time to time we experience blessed silence for a few seconds, until the next vehicle whines along, either somewhere far away or up close and personal. And in those few seconds of silence are the value of living in the country; in the city is constant artificial sound/noise.

Odd that, with my hearing not what it used to be, I would write about the joy of silence, since living in silence is a gnawing fear for any lover of words and music. Not being able to hear or comprehend the voices is a frightening prospect, but being in a place where silence reigns is joyful. No – not silence, but the absence of mechanical sounds, a place where the breeze is not drowned out, a place where the breeze can be heard and attended.

GLADNESS IS INFECTIOUS

Going from here to there

I stopped in the middle of the living room and realized I had the day to myself to do anything I wanted.

At that moment I just wanted to stop and appreciate the quiet and the day off.

GLADNESS IS INFECTIOUS

quite here in the moments

The wonder of this moment
that is here and will never come again,
overflowing with oh so much life
the sunshine and the color
and the silence (or
the chitter-chat)
of so much everything
all around

the soft of golden retriever
sprawled across the hallway fast asleep
to spring up with anticipation at a rustle

Oh Lord such all of it racing through my head
too much and not enough

i run through fields of memory around
tracks of yesterday four miles now
and away we go to where i always wished

. . .

i reach for another metaphor but it
has fled, the moment passed,

GLADNESS IS INFECTIOUS

and around the house machines churn their churn
while
    i reach for what has been instead of —
    instead of — why, here's another moment
    and another
    and another

    and see how much the purple and
    dark coneflowers and the splendid compass
    flowers on stalks high over my head burst
    yellow against blue
    and clouds that form nothing
    and all of it there — right
    up beyond in the sky

    I fill my lungs with lilac
    and breathe out new tomorrow in a sigh —

GLADNESS IS INFECTIOUS

On waking

There, did you see it, just then?

I napped like death for an hour and a half this afternoon, and you almost slipped out without my knowing, but you whispered my name to be sure, and I heard.

Now, alone, I breathe full and deep and feel the life renewed from sleep, rested and recreated anew, the cycle continued for another few precious hours.

And a truth slipped coyly through the mist — I saw it; did you? An almost-smile crossed its honest face, and I felt it sigh in wonder as it passed.

The best question in the world

I've read many a book on writing and most of them say, "Writers write. So write," and many others say, "Remember to have fun," and I've found that when I remember that sage advice, results seem to result.

And so I've been writing lately and trying to remember to have fun, and the stories are starting to emerge from the ether. I'm starting to have fun again. This is the writing I've always wanted to write — the learning how the world is, and the finding how it happens, and the trying out to see what I can make happen — not "This is what I saw last night" but "This is what I see today, and tomorrow." Write into the future, write into the mystery, discover what is and what will be, wielding naught but a pen and a keyboard, and find what's next.

"What's next?" is the best question in the world.

What are you afraid of — really? Write the fear out of existence. What do you hope? Write the hope into existence. This is the power of words, make no mistake.

Or: DO make mistakes. Stumble and stagger over the words until you find a way to lay them down smooth as newly paved highway. Write and write until your mind is weary and your fingers ache but you know you said what you came to say, even when you didn't know what you came to say until you said it.

GLADNESS IS INFECTIOUS

That's the way it is sometimes: You're just busting to get something out but you don't know what it is, so you just keep writing until, mercy me, all of a sudden it comes out and it's there and can't be taken back but it's oh so true, truer than any words you ever said before, right down there on the page.

What's next? You'll find out when you write the next sentence, and the one after that, until it's not "next" anymore, it's now and here, here and now. Yep.

Two ways to look at it all

Life's a bitch and then you die.

Or:

Life's a rollicking adventure filled with triumph and despair, thrills and chills, and in the end you leave the theater and say, "Wow, now that was a story."

May my work feed that second narrative as often and as much as I can muster.

It's all in the attitude

Oh, bother. Oh, woe. Will inspiration ever strike? It's so ha-ard to sit here and try to write. How am I going to get my characters out of this mess? It takes so long to work it all out. I don't want to sit at this desk and try to concentrate on all this.

"Isn't this great?!"

What? No. Are you crazy?

"Only crazy about how much fun I'm having. It's so great to take a little time for inspiration to strike."

You call this fun?

"Yes! Yes! Yes! It's so much fun to just sit and try to write. How am I going to get my characters out of this mess? I can take my time to work it all out. I just love to sit at this desk and concentrate on all this. I'm living the creative! Wheeeeeee!!!"

(Guess which attitude is more fun – and more productive.)

The call of the writer

I had an epiphany the other day while reading a book about the professional writing life:

Writing is not work.

Work is dragging your butt into the office or into the car to drive somewhere you'd rather not be.

Work may even be forcing yourself to sit down at the keyboard or take up some other writing tool.

But once the writing begins, it is fun, it's a challenge, it's a puzzle to be solved, a mystery to be cracked.

Sitting down to write may be work. Forcing myself to focus may be work.

But once the words start flowing, it's a river of fun, a gusher of joy, a knowing I am doing what I am meant to do, a contentment of being where I'm supposed to be, and a wondering why I fought so hard to put my body and mind in a position to be answering the call I felt all along.

GLADNESS IS INFECTIOUS

A morning of snooty snobbery

I opened my old college textbook *The Literature of England* at random yesterday morning and found "This Lime-Tree Bower My Prison," Samuel Taylor Coleridge's poem composed in his garden under a lime tree while his visiting friends took a walk in the nearby countryside. He had to stay behind, having been sidelined when his wife accidentally spilled boiling milk on his foot. (Ow-ow-ow!)

Before that, I took a brief stab at "Troilus and Criseyde," and what a surprise, 45-plus years of not reading Middle English has rendered Chaucer's brilliant quasi-epic poem essentially unreadable to me. I do know that reading it was one of the surprise delights of my education, but I would need to be re-educated to re-experience the joy — although perhaps that would be a more worthwhile venture than the three episodes of *The Blacklist* that I viewed the night before.

(Somewhere in the last few days, I read a reference that a society constantly exposed to tawdry crap aimed at the lowest common denominator becomes tawdry and low and full of crap. It was written more elegantly than that, but it was a good point. There are delights in the old stuff more subtle than a gun to the face.)

I don't mean to be a snooty snob, but I do like a turn of phrase. Discovering Coleridge's poem was another

GLADNESS IS INFECTIOUS

reminder of the thousands of undiscovered treasures waiting within reach on the shelves in this little room. OK, many of them I have indeed discovered and decided to save (Bradbury, Doc Savage, Hawthorne), but so many pages are as yet untapped, and the old treasures are fun to revisit.

Notice when I reach for examples, I pick Hawthorne (everyone knows he's a classic, although he's not necessarily many people's "favorite" classic author), Bradbury (becoming a classic but not considered so until well into his career), and Doc Savage (not "literature").

I do seem to have a unique perspective on what constitutes good reading. I enjoy enjoying stuff that's off the beaten track. I like that about being in this skin.

Exploring the piles of treasure is entertaining and instructive. "You need to get out more," they say, but, see here, we need to get in more, too. Look what I've found in here just this morning, after all.

GLADNESS IS INFECTIOUS

Journey to Far Metaphor

Reach for the stars: A man's reach must exceed his grasp, or what's a metaphor?

A story is a living thing: It begins, goes on an adventure, and comes to an end. Along the way are expectations, unexpected twists, and – if it goes well enough – a resolution and satisfying conclusion, for who wants a life, metaphorical or otherwise, that does not end well?

Make your life a page-turner

This is the dawn. This is the turning of the page. This is the new beginning, halfway through or three-quarters through or one-third through or re-doing after a false start.

Don't worry if you have turned the page before and here we go again. Do you know how many pages are in a book?

A compelling book is called a page-turner, right? Keep turning the page until the story has hooked you, until your story is so compelling we can't put it down, and you can't put it down.

Turn the page! Let's see what happens next!!

GLADNESS IS INFECTIOUS

Grant me the serenity

Now, see, this is why it's not a good idea to look at the glowing screen first thing in the morning.

I walk out with Willow to see to her morning constitutional, and it's a beautiful morning, so quiet and still that the rooster's crowing a half-mile away is clear as day, and the reverberations from a hunter's shot way in the distance can be heard to the last echo.

No wind, and therefore no crashing waves from the bay below us, no traffic on the highway — quiet stillness pervades.

I come inside and peek at social media, and crash! One of my acquaintances is bragging about how he confronted a store manager for not forcing his customers to wear masks. And that's just the beginning. Anger, fear, resentment and shaming pervade.

Outdoors, I found refuge from the storm. Isn't that just how life can be?

Just write anything until you write something

There are a number of things you can do with a blank piece of paper, or a blank screen.

You can stare at it.

You can write on it.

You can draw on it.

(You can also make paper airplanes and origami, but for purposes of this post, we'll stick with things that involve writing implements.)

Staring at it is the least productive option. Staring usually involves mental paralysis, perhaps even fear that you or I will have nothing worthwhile to say.

And you know how I sabotaged the process just then?

By tossing in that innocuous-sounding word "worthwhile."

Because if you're all balled up because you can't think of ANYTHING to say, you just threw up a second roadblock by saying it not only has to be ANYTHING, it has to be WORTHWHILE.

If you're in a place where you want to write/create something and you just feel stuck, the best thing to do is just anything. Write something, even if you end up writing, "I can't think of anything to write!" Because then you've successfully written seven words. Now write the next sentence. Then, write the next sentence after that. You've already written something, and if you keep writing, at some point you may even find yourself writing something worthwhile.

But under no circumstances can you keep staring at a blank screen until you give up. Just write anything until you accidentally write something.

This post is an example of how this works.

I was staring at a blank screen, wondering I would share for this blog this morning. My mind was almost as blank as the screen.

So ...

I wrote, "There are a number of things you can do with a blank piece of paper, or a blank screen."

And the rest followed.

GLADNESS IS INFECTIOUS

The infectiousness of gladness

What if we spent a day starting every sentence with "I'm so glad ..."?

I'm so glad I ...

I'm so glad you ...

I'm so glad we ...

How soon would we run out of things to be glad about? or would we discover, at length, that the supply is endless?

I can't help thinking people would be a lot happier if they were always looking for what makes them glad.

I'm so glad I thought of this.

GLADNESS IS INFECTIOUS

Glad ... for words

I'm so glad I ... learned to read and write. The world opened.

I learned about shy stegosauruses and buried treasure, superpowered heroes and heroines from other worlds and down the street, and with pencil and paper I created my own world.

Words give us a portal into other minds and souls, times and places. We walk with Thoreau through Walden Woods in 1854, go whale hunting with Melville in 1851, settle into the audience at the Globe Theatre in 1603 to see what story this fellow Shakespeare has come up with now.

The twisting and shouting of everyday life and social media settles into a calm between the covers of a book, and we see the more reasoned background of hastily or imprecisely spoken words. Or our hearts are hastened by the passions on the page.

We live in a world where all of these words are at our fingertips. It's a grand time to be alive.

GLADNESS IS INFECTIOUS

Glad ... for music

I'm so glad I ... hear the music.

When I was a kid I was obsessed with Top 40 radio, but I also hoarded my dad's 78 rpm records and fell in love with Artie Shaw's "Frenesi" and Benny Goodman's "Sing Sing Sing" and Raymond Scott's "Powerhouse."

My background music as I type this is Anoushka Shankar, and I seem to write most efficiently to Ahmad Jamal, but Bruce Springsteen and the Beatles and Rachael Price and Jason Mraz have been known to accompany my fingers as they tap along ... and of course the likes of Beethoven and Bach and Strauss and Copeland.

We have wind chimes hanging outside the window to my office year-round, so I hear music without melody whenever the slightest breeze or the heartiest gale is underway out there.

I am pleased to report I even hear the music in a work like "Revolution 9" by the Beatles, with its rhythms and mighty crescendos.

I think it was Terry Pratchett who had one of his characters say, "Music is everywhere if you know how to listen." And so it is.

I pity the ones who only hear noise, because there is music everywhere, ready and willing to unite us in peace. Some days I feel like I'm the only one who hears it, but that's the lie the noisemakers would have us believe.

GLADNESS IS INFECTIOUS

Glad ... for life

It's all turned around and inside out today.

I usually sit down in my blue chair to journal before dawn, but this has been one of those "everything got away from me" weeks, and so I'm writing these words a couple of hours after sunset, or about 12 hours behind. (Actually, I haven't been in the chair all week, so maybe I'm a day and a half behind, or more.)

Having a cup of coffee after supper is odd. Red is off to town doing something Christmassy, so the house is as quiet as 6 a.m.

I'm working on being grateful this week. It's easy to focus on losses and lack and how life could be better and would be easier and should be more free — the coulda-woulda-shouldas.

But then there was the couple we knew and loved who said the secret of their happiness was they decided to be content with whatever life brought their way. Their goal in life was to revel in what they had, including each other. Anything more would be a bonus and a blessing.

So I'm more than happy to have this chair to sit in, in a small but comfortable house we built in the country eight years ago, with the heat on, the light bill paid, and a tasty bluegrass band playing on the stereo.

What more could I want? Oh, I want a lot of things, most of all the discipline to finish my novels and such,

GLADNESS IS INFECTIOUS

but this year I've finally developed the discipline to blog every day, and that's a start, isn't it?

And now, to finish this oh-so-interesting year, I'm cultivating the discipline to blog every day about being glad and grateful.

What I've rediscovered is that if you go looking around for what's good about this life, it's just as easy to find stuff as it is if you try to find things to grouse about.

This of all seasons is meant to be a season of joy, so I'm grateful. I'm glad to be alive in this time, and not just because "it beats the alternative."

Look around for reasons to be glad today. I think you'll agree it feels better.

GLADNESS IS INFECTIOUS

Glad ... for independent thought

I'm so glad we ... have reason and free will.

Moms used to say, "If everyone else jumped off a cliff, would you do it, too?" and that was how we knew we didn't have to do what everyone else does.

Moms would say things like you have two ears and one mouth and you should use them in that proportion. Or look before you leap. Or if you don't have anything nice to say, don't say anything (wow, we could sure use THAT mom these days).

Nowadays sometimes it feels like moms are saying, "Jump off that cliff! It was good enough for me and your father, so it will be good enough for you."

But we still don't have to do what everyone else does.

We still get to peer over the edge of the cliff and choose to stay up here on high ground.

I don't have my mom to talk to anymore. She would have been 97 this week, but she only got 82 years and change.

She's still around, though. This whole series of "choose to be glad" musings is because when people started getting angry with each other, she would start singing, "Happy talk, keep talking happy talk," or "You'll find that life is still worthwhile if you'll just smile," or you get the picture.

GLADNESS IS INFECTIOUS

Thanks, Mom, for raising me to think happy thoughts and not necessarily doing what everyone else is doing.

If the substance between your ears is telling you that you don't want to do or say or think what everyone else is doing or saying or thinking, that's the beauty of this life: You don't have to.

Oh, you may have to suffer some consequences, like dealing with people who look at you cross-eyed and wonder why you're not doing or saying or thinking like they are.

But you're thinking for yourself. And doing what's right according to your thoughts. And saying what you think is right.

And I bet you'll sleep better tonight for it.

GLADNESS IS INFECTIOUS

Glad ... for optimism

I'm so glad ... I can see the bright side.

I confess. I'm Pollyanna.

I have done my best to cultivate an inner attitude that it's going to be all right. I've been grateful for that attitude a lot, lately.

It's a big, scary world with people who seem hell-bent on keeping it scary for as long as possible.

The scariest are the people who believe they're scaring us for our own good. People with altruistic motives are more likely to do something horrible because they believe they're acting in our best interests, to save us from something even more horrible.

People who choose the lesser of two evils are still choosing evil.

I have done my best to cultivate an inner attitude that it's always possible to choose good, if we look hard enough.

Choosing the right way is often harder than choosing the lesser of two evils, but it's more likely to result in a viable and sustainable long-term solution.

The key is to keep looking, refusing the easy and evil path, until you find that better way.

I try to expect good from people until they give me a reason to expect otherwise. It makes me more vulnerable, but I find it's worth the risk more often than not.

GLADNESS IS INFECTIOUS

How much heavier my heart would be if I expected the worst from people all the time. Politicians are like that, and tyrants — but I repeat myself.

Optimism — expecting the best, trusting other people — is a risky and potentially dangerous way to live (in many situations "cautious optimism" is the best policy), but I choose it over pessimism as often as I can.

Sure, pessimists expect the worst and are pleasantly surprised from time to time, but I'd rather be constantly on the lookout for the best in people, in situations, and in life in general.

Hope is just easier on the soul.

GLADNESS IS INFECTIOUS

Glad ... for a favorite pen

I'm so glad I ... found this pen.

As I continue my season of gladness, I look at my hand and remember how grateful I am that I discovered its near-perfect match, wow, probably more than 10 years ago now.

Something about the way the Uni-Ball Jetstream Sport fit in my hand was more comfortable than any pen I'd ever owned. The ink flowed smoothly and I could write for a long time without my hand getting tired.

I don't know if it's the greatest pen ever made, but it's the greatest pen for my individual hand.

Unfortunately I must be a very small market, because the next time I went to the office supply store, I found them in the clearance section. The clerk said that probably meant they were discontinued.

I did what any convert would do: I bought out the store. Then I went online and got a case.

That turned out to be an overreaction, because they were NOT discontinued, or if they were the company brought them back, because if you do a quick search you can find them still for sale.

But at least I have a supply that will last my lifetime, even if I manage to live as long as my dad did, which would be almost 30 more years for me.

GLADNESS IS INFECTIOUS

Maybe it's silly to spend words of gratitude on an inexpensive pen, or maybe that's the whole point of searching for reasons to be glad: Some of the most amazing reasons are very simple and everyday.

GLADNESS IS INFECTIOUS

Glad ... for winter solstice

I'm so glad ... for the promise of light.

By the time most folks read this, the winter solstice will have occurred (unless you're in the southern hemisphere, in which case hello! and happy summer solstice) — I'm told the solstice happens at 4:02 a.m. CST this Monday, Dec. 21, 2020.

Up until this morning, the amount of sunlight reaching us northerners has been decreasing by increments every day, until there is a mere 7 hours, 48 minutes between sunrise and sunset.

Humans need light. It's no fun when the sun is illuminating our lives less than one-third of the time.

That's why I'm so glad for the winter solstice. Starting today, the amount of sunlight will be INCREASING by increments every day.

Oh, sure, it's going to get colder and snowier for a while. But slowly and surely, we'll have more light to navigate the winter, day by day.

I think that's why Christians chose this time of year to celebrate the birth of someone who was to bring light to a dark world: because it's literally going to get brighter from now on.

Every December we have the solace of solstice: No matter how dark everything may seem right now, from now on every day will bring just a little more light, until that magic day in June when the sun is shining almost two-thirds of the time.

Then we'll have that bittersweet season when it's warm and comfortable outside but slowly getting darker, but the shorter days are a gentle reminder to prepare for the coming cold months.

And then we'll be back at a day like this one, when light is a precious commodity.

But be assured: More light is coming.

GLADNESS IS INFECTIOUS

Glad ... for the Bill of Rights

I'm so glad we ... live in the place where the Bill of Rights was drafted.

Imagine a world so dark and oppressive that someone had to draft such a document.

The First Amendment alone is a masterwork that sets down five essential unalienable rights that should have been self-evident, but apparently they weren't because they had to write them down.

"Congress shall make no law respecting an establishment of religion, or prohibiting the free exercise thereof; or abridging the freedom of speech, or of the press; or the right of the people peaceably to assemble, and to petition the government for a redress of grievances."

Imagine a world where someone had to document that:

Government has no right to set up an official state religion or otherwise interfere with your ability to worship in the manner you choose;

Government has no right to say you can't speak your mind;

Government has no right to keep you from writing and publishing as you please;

GLADNESS IS INFECTIOUS

Government has no right to keep you from gathering for a peaceful purpose; and

Government has no right to ignore your complaints about what it's doing — it has to listen and consider remedies.

And that's just the beginning! The Bill of Rights sets down that the government can't stop you from taking measures for self-defense, it can't arrest or detain you without cause, it can't search you or your property without justification, it can't lock you up and throw away the key — oh, and my favorite, there's a line in there that just because one of your rights isn't on the list, it doesn't mean you don't have that right.

Imagine a government so nasty that someone had to write down all of these reminders.

Eh, err, what's that? You don't have to imagine? Well, then, I'm even more glad.

Imagine a world where nobody thought to stand up to tyrants and say, "Hey, buddy, you can't do that to us."

The Bill of Rights was passed Dec. 15, 1791, and we've been having conversations about it ever since, most of them starting with one of us waving the document and saying, "Hey buddy, you can't ..."

And as long as we're having those conversations, there's hope for us all.

GLADNESS IS INFECTIOUS

Glad ... for serendipity

I'm so glad we ... had a serendipitous miscommunication.

I've been enjoying an early Christmas present — Paul McCartney's *New* album, that is to say, the album McCartney released in 2014 called *New*.

A couple of weeks ago, Red asked me what I want for Christmas, I was stumped for a moment, and then I said, "Well, Paul McCartney has a new album coming out."

That ended that discussion, until the other day when I casually remarked, "Well, Paul McCartney's new album came out today."

She gave me a curious look and said, "Uh oh, I think I may have made a mistake," reaching under the tree and giving me a brightly wrapped box to see if she had.

Yep. Not being as tuned to (or interested in) pop culture as I am, she didn't know I was talking about *McCartney III*, which was to be released Dec. 18. She just did a search for "New Paul McCartney album," and the rest is now history.

We had a good chuckle, and I'm now playing *New* through for the third time. It has some very tasty stuff in it.

And as Christmas presents go, it's more fun to get a surprise gift I love than exactly what I asked for. That's the joy of serendipity.

Glad ... for what ifs

I'm so glad ... for speculative fiction.

Of course, ALL fiction is speculative. There are science fiction and fantasy what-ifs ...

What if a farm boy in a distant galaxy grew up to be a new hope? (*Star Wars*)

What if a farm girl accidentally traveled to a magical kingdom and saved her friends? (*The Wizard of Oz*)

... but all stories begin with "What if."

What if a shallow rich girl was caught up in a war and had to defend her mansion along? (*Gone With The Wind*)

What if a cynical bar owner met the woman who broke him and found out her side of the story? (*Casablanca*)

What if a sad man on the brink of suicide had a chance to see how much he means to people? (*It's A Wonderful Life*)

What if a little girl in a racist town saw her attorney father defend an innocent man? (*To Kill a Mockingbird*)

I've had people say they tend not to like speculative fiction. But every story is speculative fiction: What if this happened? What if he met her? What if he met her again years later? What if they returned to the scene of their triumph? or their most bitter loss? What if someone

GLADNESS IS INFECTIOUS

was murdered? What if some developer wanted to tear down the old town hall?

If you like good stories, you like speculative fiction.

GLADNESS IS INFECTIOUS

Choose gratitude

Oh, it's so so easy, these days especially, to be caught up in alarm and anger and fear and blame and woe. Another choice is always available.

I wrote in my journal last night about my worries and concerns, expecting to transcribe them into today's blog post, but I couldn't get to sleep, so I got up and wrote this instead.

At least one animal has lived with me for more than 40 years now, ever since that black cat moved in. During that time three special puppies bonded with me; their names are Poppins and Tucker and Willow, and those who knew me at various times (or know me now) recognize at least one of those names. I can't imagine caring for a furry friend more than I love Willow, but I do remember having deep feelings for Pops and Tuck.

It's easy to forget, in the rush of all that happens in daily life, how much we have in our lives to be grateful for. I am forever grateful for the peaceful joy of a quiet moment with Willow. I am so glad to have such a sweet soul under our roof to remind me to choose love first.

GLADNESS IS INFECTIOUS

You say you want a resolution

National Novel Writing Month (NaNoWriMo) is an exercise that comes around every November, where participants pledge to themselves and each other that they will aim to write a novel of 50,000 words or more in 30 days.

It works out to 1,666 words per day, which does not sound daunting until it looms like a target in the distance. But every year thousands of folks discover that if they set their minds to it, they can produce 1,666 words a day and eventually 50,000 words in a month.

And what's next? (That Magical Question)

Well, Steven Pressfield likes to tell the story of how he finished his first novel at last, and he went running to celebrate with his mentor, whose reaction was along the lines of "Good for you! Start on the next one today."

The mentor is right. The point of NaNoWriMo is to prove you can do it, if not in 30 days, then eventually. For some, I suppose, that's the whole point. But for the people who want to write, the proof is simply the first step — and "what's next" is realizing that it's a sustainable process.

Why wait until November to start writing a 50,000-word novel in 30 days? Why wait until the first of any month? You can start now.

GLADNESS IS INFECTIOUS

This is the time of year that people talk about setting goals and resolutions. But why set goals based on the calendar? What is so magical about doing something by Nov. 30 or Dec. 31, or starting on Nov. 1 or Jan. 1?

You can start today, right this minute, and you can finish by Jan. 23 or May 4 or whenever.

Start when you're ready. Set a deadline, but finish when you're done — maybe that'll be a month before deadline (better) or a month after (not as good, but still finished).

Resolve to do it now, not "in the new year." If it's worth doing then, it's worth doing asap.

GLADNESS IS INFECTIOUS

The zen of coffee

Sometimes I have the foresight to make coffee before I go to bed. I load the water in the tank, pile the coffee grounds in the basket, and apply a sticky note to the front of the machine to remind me that all I have to do is press the "on" button to start the brew the next morning.

There came a morning when I was tired of it all. I dragged myself out of bed out of a sense of obligation and dragged myself around the house, resentful that I wasn't still dreaming strange adventures or lost in oblivion, and generally ready to retire except for the fact that I had "real-world" obligations hanging over my head.

I grumbled into the kitchen and was caught short by the little sign on the coffee machine.

JUST PRESS ON.

Oh. Right.

There will always come a morning (it could be any time of day, but it always feels like morning) when you're ready to quit, chuck it all, stop doing what you're doing, end the misery — and if there's something about those feeling that feels like defeat, then, oh yes, it's because it *is* defeat.

"You only fail if you stop writing," my mentor-I-never-met Ray Bradbury said. And it's true: You're not really defeated until you quit.

GLADNESS IS INFECTIOUS

If you find yourself stuck or miserable and wishing you were anywhere else than pursuing your life's dream — because I sincerely hope at some point what you are doing did have something to do with pursuing your dreams — just press on. Keep going.

That's the way to push through the malaise and misery and find yourself in a better mood. If you just press on, at some point something will remind you why you wanted to do this, maybe even reignite the spark and push you to a new dream beyond the first one.

Just press on.

At the very least, maybe you'll get coffee out of it.

Let it never be said

Let it never be said that it never be said.

Let no thought be condemned to disappear because it was too much to bear.

Foul thoughts, bottled up, tend to fester and grow even more foul if not let out into the air and allowed to mingle with clearer and saner fare.

Am I advocating for unfettered ugly speech? No. I'm advocating for a conversation where the ugly can be met with beauty, or at least with anti-ugly. Free speech means you can say whatever you like, freely and honestly, but you have to be willing to allow a free and honest response.

Let sunshine cleanse the dark and chase it with healthy rebuke, rather than let the dark simmer and grow strong.

GLADNESS IS INFECTIOUS

I believe ...

... in the power of music.

... in happy endings.

... in the decency of most humans.

... that peace is more powerful than war mongers.

... that Willow is finally ready to go to sleep.

GLADNESS IS INFECTIOUS

Remember to play

A cup of coffee. A half-dozen Biscoff cookies to dunk, absorbing the liquid to create a sweet treat. A cat bounding onto the chair's arm with an interested meow. This is how it starts.

The first day of school for kids is a symbolic new beginning for grownups, too. For those grownups who may have forgotten the importance of preserving your kid-ness, the first day of school is a reminder to get back in touch with that young person who has been hibernating in your bones.

My younger self would sit cross-legged on the bed, scribbling song lyrics and poems or drawing comic-book adventures for my own amusement — or my brothers' or friends' amusement — over the years the songs and poems I grew less ready to share, and later more. But I would always be creating something in my fantasy world, with my stable of superheroes, and my Top 40 of songs that I made up, written and drawn and sung by people whose names I made up, too. The high school poems were the first I assigned my own name to, and then it was "w.p. bluhm," because I loved what e.e. cummings did to a page.

Dance like no one is watching — that thought emerges from a few moments of reflection abut how those youthful efforts were created without much care

GLADNESS IS INFECTIOUS

for who would see or hear them (but saved just in case some posterity would want to see them — or saved because they are the singular creations of w.p. bluhm and therefore unique to the universe and irreplaceable if not priceless) — Write like no one is looking over your shoulder and criticizing and shocked that such a thing came from your mind. Never you mind who's minding, just dance. write. sing. play.

Play — that's where this started. I have forgotten to play, or rather I remember how to play but have forgotten or neglected to do so.

Now, if you'll excuse me, I'm going to go sit on the bed for a bit.

GLADNESS IS INFECTIOUS

The writing station

"Small steps are great. But you gotta keep walking."

A guest on Joanna Penn's "The Creative Penn" podcast said that some years ago, and I wrote it down and posted it above my writing station. I forgot to write down who said it, though. My bad.

At the time I didn't have a lot of free time to write for myself. The guest reminded me that it's OK to write only a little at a time, but if I want to make progress, skipping a session or quitting altogether cannot be an option.

Here's what other words of wisdom have been enshrined in Post-It notes around my writing station:

+ "Enlighten. Encourage. Entertain." — the "mission statement" of my writing career. On another Post-It note I have "Encourage. Entertain. Enlighten." I must have been in a different frame of mind that day.

+ Heinlein's Rules: 1. You must write. 2. You must finish what you start. 3. You must refrain from rewriting except to editorial order. 4. You must put it on the market. 5. You must keep it on the market until sold. (By the way, Dean Wesley Smith has a terrific short book about Heinlein's Rules, called, well, Heinlein's Rules.)

GLADNESS IS INFECTIOUS

+ (in big letters) HAVE FUN

+ "When you have a God-given talent, you must use it all the time." — Vince Lombardi

+ "Just write every day of your life. Read intensely. Then see what happens. Most of my friends who are put on that diet have very pleasant careers." — Ray Bradbury

+ "Your writing IS your real life." — Lauren Sapala

+ "Read, every day, something no one else is reading. Think, every day, something no one else is thinking. Do, every day, something no one else would be silly enough to do. It is bad for the mind to continually be part of unanimity." — Christopher Morley's last message to his friends, 1957

+ "I have a contract with my audience — that I will do better, that I will give them a reason to come in again that is more than the reason we gave them last time." — Joss Whedon

Last but not least, taped to my computer monitor right above the screen:

+ "You only fail if you stop writing." (Bradbury)

GLADNESS IS INFECTIOUS

The bad news about posting inspirational sayings at your work station is that you tend to take them for granted every once in a while, because they literally become part of the scenery.

The good news is every so often, your eyes focus on the words and give you a good jolt — "Oh yeah, I need to remember that."

Believe in yourself

What would you do if it was only you — you were all by yourself and no one was watching/reading/listening but you had to do it anyway?

That's your passion.

Someone said that once: Your passion is what you would do even if nobody cared or paid attention.

Work on getting better at that thing, and people may start to notice.

But even if they don't notice, you have to do it anyway, don't you? It's what you were meant to do — and your audience is out there somewhere.

So keep going. Keep getting better. Time will find you.

GLADNESS IS INFECTIOUS

How to overcome inertia

Write the next sentence. Take the next step.
That's all there really is to it.

GLADNESS IS INFECTIOUS

Here I sit among the detritus of human endeavor

I was born on a Sunday evening, and so I have seen 67-times-52-plus-change Sundays in my life. Do the math later if you'd like.

I have piles and piles of debris to show for it. Well, "debris" is the wrong word for what's piled in my little home office. These are shelves of books and boxes of records and magazines and various detritus of human endeavor.

Here's a 1941 Philco radio that was crafted and assembled by good hard-working folks who, I hope, proud of their work. And each book, each record, represents a lifetime — several lifetimes, in fact, because while one name or one face may appear on the cover, it is also the work of an editor, the printer, the layout and cover artists, the sound engineer, the accompanying musicians — all those hundreds and thousands of people created what is contained in this debris.

Think of the thousands of names scrolling along at the end of a film — all of those lives invested in creating a single bit of popular art.

And so I'm loathe to consign any of it to a garbage bin. As Paul Simon wrote in a tune many years ago now, "Preserve your memories; they're all that's left you."

GLADNESS IS INFECTIOUS

Reflections while sitting in a lawn chair waiting for an eBay delivery watching the traffic fly by

2:20 p.m. 9-21-2020

Hello, hello, hello, everyone! In less than a minute you will be a mile away and wondering if you really saw a white-haired man in a lawn chair, leg crossed to reveal bare ankles and slippers, otherwise wearing office clothes and writing in a red journal with a pen.

Where are you going, anyway? People come and go so quickly here, off to the Emerald City along a yellow, brick road, dump trucks loaded with soil and campers loaded with people, and the tinge of orange in the trees across the highway reminds one and all that tomorrow is the first day of autumn.

We have so much in common, you and I and all of us, as we rush from here to there bearing witness to what we have seen and what we hope to be. I wish we could focus more on our dreams and desires and not so much on our skin-deep differences.

We are each of us alone, no two exactly alike, and we share a desire to be left alone, to be free to live our lives in peace, but something-less-than-peace is thrust upon us constantly. Peace, then, is a fleeting joy, felt in a southerly breeze that rustles the trees on the last day of

GLADNESS IS INFECTIOUS

summer, focused on endings rather than beginnings even though (as the song says) they are one and the same.

What begins here, in this hour when one season is drawing to a close and another approaching? What begins today, as leave turn to more vivid colors than green and — even though right now it is warm and comfortable — experience tells us the chill is inevitable someday soon? Every day, every moment holds promise if you seek it out. Every day, every moment holds finality if you look for it.

Billions of people interacting with each other, trillions of life forms interacting, lead to infinite combinations, so of course beginnings and endings are always within reach — beginnings and endings as birth and death or as commonplace as beginning a new journal page or the end of an eBay package's journey from shipping box to mailbox, which is the reason I'm sitting in our driveway waiting for the mail carrier, so I can sop up some sunshine and save the carrier a few steps up the walk.

And the travelers who rushed past when I started writing are now as much as 30 miles away.

GLADNESS IS INFECTIOUS

The cycle and the sharing

Fear not, lass. It has been this cold before, and the leaves have fallen off the trees, and the waters have risen this high, and the deserts have grown so parched – and then the warm comes, and the leaves grow, and the waters recede, and rains come.

It is a cycle, you see, and nothing good or bad continues and remains unchanging. Do not fear the change, but prepare for the next phase of the cycle. Understand the patterns and don't be alarmed when the change comes. Night follows day, cold follows warmth and back to cold and back to warm.

We breathe in, we breathe out, the blood pump contracts and relaxes, contracts and relaxes.

The best we can do is the best we can do until we can't anymore – Oh, and if someone tells you that you can't anymore, and you know perfectly well that you still can, well, then, don't waste too much time arguing, just go to someone else somewhere and give your gifts to them.

We are built to give; we receive through our giving and sharing. Empty is the soul who is not allowed to give, emptier still the soul who will not give, for they are filled to bursting with gifts to share, gifts designed to be shared, and the gifts must go somewhere: Unshared, they

GLADNESS IS INFECTIOUS

disappear to oblivion instead of into the universe where they belong.

Better to be forgotten, waiting to be rediscovered and restored, than to have never used and shared the gifts God and/or the universe placed in your soul.

Tell me what you've got: Let's share each other's gifts.

A dog's life

Dejah Thoris, Princess of Mars, stirs in her sleep, curled in a chair, her flag of a tail brushing her nose. Does she dream of running miles and miles, making friends with everyone she meets and eating everything that moves? Is she sad because she spends so much time in a house full of comfortable places to sleep but not exactly full of crazy things to do while waking? Does she think we need more crazy things to do, or is sleeping and dreaming of wild adventures enough? She is not wanting of where her next meal will come from, which makes her more fortunate than millions.

"It's a dog's life," people complain sometimes, and I'm not sure that's such a bad thing. There are days I would like nothing more than to curl up and dream all day.

Autumn sunshine and the promise of snow

The sun is back today. Yesterday was Gray close your eyes and rest in the gloom, and today is slowly building into Look at all the glory come and run in the light — although now the green is starting to fade to yellow and red in anticipation of future brown.

On days like today, everything looks like potential, although deadlines are hinted in the approaching fall colors. Many of the tasks at hand ought to be done before it's too cold to be outside comfortably for long – and so we're talking a couple of months to do them – others must be completed before the work involves tramping and digging through snow.

It's hard to imagine snow on a day like this – just as in a few months it will be hard to imagine green and flowers and a warm breeze from the south and ice cream melting in our hands. It's the circle of seasons, time marching on and opportunities rising and being missed all in a row.

Let today be the one (or one of many) where opportunity is seized and grappled into life.

GLADNESS IS INFECTIOUS

Invocation

Are you there, Muse? It's me, Warren. I straggled out of bed before light to see if we could have a chat. They say showing up is half the battle, but I think it's more like three quarters, because I know for a fact that you're not going to show up unless I do. So here I am, and here we go, right?

It's kind of fascinating that people are OK with invoking the Muse or Mother Nature or the Spirit of Gaea but get uncomfortable with the idea of God, who could be all of the above. Maybe it's their idea of who God is, or how the concept of God has been co-opted over the years, seeing as they're just fine with the idea of Someone or Something supernatural and bigger than us.

I had more than one dream last night that I was sure I'd remember this morning because they were so vivid and interesting. More water under the spilled milk, um, more crying over the bridge — hmmm, looks like I need my morning dose of caffeine.

That which has dissipated into the ether likely will return someday, disguised as something new. I find myself finding old blog posts where I said something I thought I'd thought for the first time just recently. I guess it's a variation on "There's nothing new under the sun": There's nothing new in my latest thoughts.

GLADNESS IS INFECTIOUS

(The Muse and I had a marvelous conversation after this. I promise to share it someday.)

Realization

Today is full of promise first thing in the morning and full of regret or satisfaction at sunset. Tomorrow is a wish and Yesterday a vague memory, but Today is where the energy resides.

Today you can act – Yesterday you either did or didn't, and Tomorrow you might, but Today you can.

Even better: "I'm going to do it today" is good, but it's still just a promise. "I'm going to act Now" is most powerful. You're acting Now; it's happening Now.

Understand? Now – is. You reach for a coffee cup, lift it to your lips, and draw the warm comfort down your throat – Now. The moment passes, and you acted or you didn't, but it's still Now, whatever that means to you.

Now. Today. while the power is in your hands. You have no direct power over Tomorrow, and Yesterday is out of your control. Only Now do you realize.

Realize = To make real.

Further realization

I'm still reeling a bit over my realization about the word realize.

When you finalize something, you make it final. It wasn't final to you before, that it to say, it wasn't what you understood to be complete.

When you realize something, you make it real. It wasn't real before, that is to say, it wasn't part of what you understood about reality.

I just realized.

It's fun, to me, to discover new nuances about familiar old words and gain a deeper understanding about their meaning.

Sometimes the discovery is a correction, as the time I referred to a colleague as my "erstwhile" co-worker, having always understood it as a synonym for "esteemed," only to learn the word may indeed refer to an esteemed colleague but more accurately refers to a former colleague.

And sometimes, as this time, it simply tells where the word came from. I always knew what realize means but I hadn't noticed its kinship to finalize, with the "ize" performing essentially the same function in both cases.

Your reaction may be, "Yeah, so?" What can I say? I'm a word nerd. Are you just now realizing that?

GLADNESS IS INFECTIOUS

Up through the time machine

I met some old friends for conversation last night, and they each offered me an insight or two.

"Life asks for rewards back because it has favored us with animation," Ray said, encouraging me to leave something for posterity to chew on.

Henry was in a reminiscent mood, and he hummed me an old Lapland song with the refrain, "A boy's will is the wind's will, and the thoughts of youth are long, long thoughts."

And Ed, always the mysterious one, told me, "love is the every only god" and went on to explain, and he was right as always.

It mattered not that Ray told me this in 1990, and Henry in 1858, and Ed in 1940. All three of them are not especially mobile these days, but they left their words for safekeeping, and I traveled through time to retrieve them.

I suspect this is one reason we write books: to still be talking to friends after we're done talking. And so, should this combination of words happen to reach you long after I'm dust, I encourage you to be the friend that Ray, Henry and Ed have been to me, and write the future a letter.

A meal for the ages

"I'm alive, confound it," he cried, feeling mortality chill his bones. "I loved myself enough women to have a horde of offspring to keep my memory alive, but it never took, and here I am childless, no one to carry a trace of my DNA to the next generation. I failed in the prime directive to reproduce and keep the species going, so I sit here scribbling evidence that I was here in lieu of passing along my genes. I pieced these words together so that when my dust is scattered to the winds, something tangible will remain that says I lived and here is my offering to the future, not in the form of a bright young scientist or poet to save the world but words, words that if you read and absorb properly, perhaps you will learn to be what my never-born child would have been, and What I Was will live on, my white plume of honor and glory and words to live by and love by —"

"Are you quite done now?" she asked. "Can you sit down and eat your supper, or do you need to orate a bit longer?"

"I am not quite done," he conceded, "nor do I expect to be done anytime soon. I see possibilities in every sunrise and the dance of puppies chasing each other, but I also feel the glory of a sunset and the contented sigh of the old gray dog under the dining room table. Here, there is life worth preserving and sharing and loving."

GLADNESS IS INFECTIOUS

"Bully for you," she said, setting a plate of oh so very delicious looking food under his nose. "Youll live even longer if you eat something."

He looked at the food and gaped in awed pleasure. And years later, after his ashes had been scattered to the wind, the critics mourned his passing and spoke of the poetry that sang in his description of that meal.

The zen of early rising

Sometimes, pulling myself out from under the covers at 5 a.m., I resist the urge to climb back in, and instead I go to my writing/reading chair and start to write, and something pretty good comes out. It's like some force in the universe wants to keep me from seeing what I would see if I awaken, so it lulls me back to sleep. But we need to wake up and see eventually, so the universe rewards me with a bit of insight when I get up anyway.

It will be easier to do now that we have "fallen back" and 5 a.m. is what 6 a.m. was 24 hours ago. I've thought before it would be nice to live in Standard Time year-round even during those months when others live in Daylight-Saving Time, waking an hour before everyone else and living in a quiet standard world that may be darker but wits are sharper because they're refreshed and uncluttered.

"We get an extra hour of sleep tonight" — or we get to start the day an hour earlier with the same amount of sleep. That latter thought feels a bit more ... empowering perhaps.

GLADNESS IS INFECTIOUS

The awesome explosion

I have come up with a new simile to describe myself lately. It can be yours.

Every day I jump out of bed and step on a landmine. The land mine is me.

After the explosion, I spend the rest of the day putting the pieces together.

Now, it's your turn. Jump!

— Ray Bradbury, *Zen in the Art of Writing*

Boom.

He jumped out of bed and saw the possibilities, all scattered and beautiful and stretching out to the horizon.

No, don't go picking them up and examining them to death, he thought to himself, just look out at all the life.

Here is a shining star in the sky beckoning with joy and hope, here is a thought that will make someone feel more alive and ready to face whatever it is that's holding them back, here is a magic racing car that travels to other worlds, and here is an idea that no one ever thought before in quite the same way you just thought it.

My oh my, all the possibilities and potentialities and what the day could be. Which to choose? All of them!

Seize this awe and tuck it into your heart to power your day, because it's an awesome world and the more

GLADNESS IS INFECTIOUS

you respond with happy awe, the more your day will be happy and awesome.

Add to the beauty

I am approaching the end of another journal; this one has taken something more than just two months to fill, and I looked back to the early pages to find something I've already shared that bears repeating:

"Add to the beauty or add to the despair — each of us has two choices — more than two, actually, infinite choices — but each of us adds something every day."

Each day is a series of givings and receivings. We give of ourselves, and we receive what others give. May our mutual goal be to add to the beauty with our giving.

Encourage in the face of despair.

Hold a light in the darkness.

Love in the face of hate.

Laugh.

There's a rugged road, as Judee Sill sang. Meet it with hope, meet it with a stubborn intention to smooth the path for the next traveler coming along, a stubborn refusal to be ruffled by the potholes and cracks in the pavement.

Each of us adds something every day — may my contributions make it better.

GLADNESS IS INFECTIOUS

The gift of the wind chimes

I pause in my morning visit with my journal to breathe, to listen to the wind chimes outside my window, and to feel the warm coffee flow down my throat to warm my entrails.

The wind chimes are in the background almost always, because we live on a windy hill, and the song is always the same, infinite in its variety and comforting because no matter how the wind blows is the promise of music — the world's energy not exactly harnessed but borrowed (perhaps) to find music in the gentlest breeze and the harshest storm.

The wind chimes were a gift, and they are a gift to this day. Gifts are like that, aren't they? You always remember that someone gave this to you. They are a bit of someone else's soul saying, "I thought you might like this, or need this," and when they were right the memory of that person lingers with the gift for as long as you have it and longer. And if the gift was an act, the memory lives all the longer.

The wind chimes have no set melody. The melody is the wind.

GLADNESS IS INFECTIOUS

Words and music about words and music

I restrung the 12-string guitar on Sunday. First I took the nine old strings off and wiped the dust from my old friend, who had been hanging on the wall for a long time.

Something had made me wait. I looked up at her more than once in all this time, and I would take her six-stringed companion down for a few minutes now and then, but the 12-string Ensenada hung up there, the new pack of strings tucked behind the old, waiting.

I was astonished when I figured out exactly how long she had waited.

It was a bright sunny 1975 summer day in Waupaca, Wisconsin, I remember, when I walked into the music store on Main Street thinking about buying a guitar with steel strings to accompany my nylon-stringed old pal Herbie (who was fated to be stolen from a hotel parking lot in Michigan City, Indiana, two or three years later, but that's another tale, which also has a happy ending, thank you, Ed). This was to be the first major purchase of my official adulthood; I had graduated from college a few weeks earlier and had now earned enough to buy a new guitar.

I saw 12 strings and opened my mind a bit. Hmm, double the strings, double the sound, perhaps. I am an extremely bashful performer, and my main form of musical expression has been via overdubbed recordings, so I was thinking with a 12-string, I could get a bigger sound on tape with fewer overdubs. I don't recall the exact price, but the figure $79 hovers in my mind, and she came home with me, and 12 strings has been part of "my" sound ever since.

One of the first songs I learned was "Sister Golden Hair," the No. 1 hit at the time, and "Lonely People," another tune by the band called America, and they did indeed sound fuller than they did when played with just six strings — sorry, Herbie. Think of the 12-string guitar solo on "I Know I'll Never Find Another You" or the lush strumming on "You've Got to Hide Your Love Away" and you can imagine the difference that 12 strings make.

In recent years I had slowly migrated away from music, and from working with sound in general. I had produced 20 homemade albums of my songs from 1973 to 2010, and close to 250 podcast episodes from 2006 to 2016, but the microphones have been stashed away and the guitars have waited for me on the wall for — how long has it been?

I remembered that I'd ordered the new strings on Amazon, so I knew it'd be easy to find out when I bought them. Come here, lil' iPad, let's see how long the 12-string has been waiting for her 12 new strings.

GLADNESS IS INFECTIOUS

Oh. my. gaw.

"Ordered on March 23, 2014."

So: Sunday I played the 12-string guitar for the first time in six and a half years.

Oh. my. gaw.

I am pleased with myself that the first thing I wrote in my journal after making that discovery was, "It felt good. I need to rebuild the callouses (on my fingertips), but it will come. I need to relearn the songs, but they will come. I want to learn new songs, too, and make new songs. March 23, 2014. Really?"

... pleased with myself because I could have sunk into a tar pit of wondering where my music went for six and a half years, and mourned for what went missing, but instead I focused on what comes next.

Somewhere along the way I decided I'm not a great singer-songwriter and my compositions and recordings are a hobby, not a vocation, but the songs are still a part of me, markers along the way from here to there, and I'm sorry to have neglected them.

But, one of the last songs I wrote and recorded back in 2010 had the refrain, "Stop looking back; this is today."

And today, the guitar on the wall has 12 new strings, and the entry in my journal rhymes.

Let's get to play

"Let's get to work" is a common way of saying, "OK, kids, stop playing now, there's serious business to be done, no more fun."

But when we're having fun, we love what we're doing so much more than when it's drudgery.

"Let's get to play" sounds much more inviting. For the musician or the athlete, to play is to work. So it is for the rest of us, when we're in the right place.

What we become

You have heard it said, "We become what we think about." The great inspirational speaker Earl Nightingale called it The Greatest Secret, it's the basis of the book The Secret, and writer James Allen wrote a brilliant little book more than 100 years ago along those lines: As A Man Thinketh.

I want to drag one sentence out of Seth Godin's new book, *The Practice*, and suggest a corrolary.

"We become what we do."

One follows the other.

GLADNESS IS INFECTIOUS

You can do it

You can do it. That much is certain.

I am one of the blessed ones whose mom told me constantly, "I believe you are capable of doing anything you set your mind to." That encouragement helped make me what I am today and kept me going when times were tough.

"I can do this," you tell yourself, "because I can do anything I set my mind to."

Here's the secret: You really can do it. It's helpful to have a mom to remind you, but it's a simple fact of life: Whatever "it" is, you can do it.

That's actually the easy part, knowing you can do it. You really can do anything.

The hard part? the rest of the moms' affirmation of faith: You set your mind to do.

Setting your mind to do something is the most important part of the equation, because it might take years and all your strength to train your mind and body to get it done, so setting your mind for the task is the key.

But!

If you ARE willing to invest your time and energy into the learning how to do it, the awkward trying to do it and falling short, and the steadily getting better and better until you're good enough —

GLADNESS IS INFECTIOUS

Then:

You can do it. You can do anything you set your mind to.

Go ahead. Set your mind. Get started. Take the first step, then the next, and keep going. Eventually you will do it. You'll see.

GLADNESS IS INFECTIOUS

No. really.

What if you CAN do it?

Do you see how that changes everything?

"One of the great discoveries a man makes, one of the great surprises, is to find he can do what he was afraid he couldn't do."

I wish I'd said that, but Henry Ford beat me to it, a long time ago, so long ago I hadn't been born yet, and you know how long THAT is.

Ford is also the guy who said, "Whether you think you can do it, or you think you can't, you're right."

Mind set is everything.

OK, it's a big part of everything. You can believe you can do something and still not do it. I hate to admit how many times I did that, or rather didn't.

I have a Vince Lombardi quote at eye level in my work station here at home: "When you have a God-given talent, you must use it all the time."

It's sort of an obligation (hence "must"). Even back in Biblical times they would say, "To whom much is given, much will be required."

Set your mind. Believe you can do it. Go and do it. It's a simple formula. Might take a minute or it might take years, but you can do it.

Why are you still waiting? Go.

GLADNESS IS INFECTIOUS

Turns out the key really is to just do it

This is the 101st day of my 92-day challenge. Back at the end of July, to celebrate my finally getting an independent host for WarrenBluhm.com, I committed to writing a blog post every day in August, September, and October, or 92 consecutive days. I don't believe I've ever managed that.

Turns out it's as easy as deciding to do it. It's like working for a radio station that puts out nine newscasts a day, or for a daily newspaper: You put out nine newscasts every day, or one newspaper. You don't have a choice. You made the commitment, you do it.

The difference is that the newscasts and the newspapers were a commitment to other people. For better or worse, over the years I've been much better at keeping those external commitments than promises I made to myself.

Several times over the years I've written about such commitments and made big announcements — my Kaiju trilogy, my detective stories, even my superhero stories — and fallen through before the projects were completed.

So this time, I decided to just do it. I made no announcements like "This is now a daily blog." I just started blogging every day. And what do you know.

GLADNESS IS INFECTIOUS

I'm a little nervous that now I've given the game away, I'll stop shipping a post every day. But I'm trying not to dwell on that fear; after all, I'm the proud author of *Refuse to be Afraid*.

This is the flip side of telling everyone I was going to do something and not doing it: I didn't tell a soul until I could tell everyone, "Look what I did." I like this feeling better.

And I feel a lot more confident that you'll believe me when I finish by saying: See you tomorrow.

GLADNESS IS INFECTIOUS

A new dream all its own

"Smile ... Though there are clouds in the sky, you'll get by."

"You got to have a dream — If you don't have a dream, how you gonna have a dream come true?"

What do you dream, friend?

I've been having a dream of folks talking to one another like friends, and being interested in what we have in common and fascinated by the uniqueness in every living soul, and boosting what it is that makes us different but the same, and living their life to the fullest the way they choose —

because we've tried being afraid of one another, and hating people who are different, and forcing our will on each other, and hurting, and yelling, and killing, and look where that got us.

"I come in peace," that's the mantra, and I go in peace, and we leave each other alone, unless you need my help, and then I'll do what I can.

I'm not sure how to get this dream to come true. I think it starts with a smile.

Who am I again? (author's note)

I live in Door County not far from the shores of Green Bay, Wisconsin, with my wife Red, two golden retrievers – Willow The Best Dog There Is™ and Dejah Thoris, Princess of Mars – and Blackberry the cat.

I (1953-) was raised in New Jersey but fell in love at first sight with the blue skies of Wisconsin, where I have spent my entire adulthood, first in radio news, then as a reporter/editor of community newspapers, more recently incorporating creative writing and book publishing into that mix.

In addition to being the mild-mannered editor of a local community paper and owner-operator of a local independent online news site, I am the author of *How to Play a Blue Guitar*, *A Bridge at Crossroads*, *Refuse to be Afraid*, the Myke Phoenix series of novelettes, *A Scream of Consciousness*, and the science-fiction novellas *The Imaginary Bomb* and *The Imaginary Revolution*.

I blog every day at WarrenBluhm.com

I also have an irregular newsletter that you can join here. Share your email address (I'll never re-share it) and I'll give you a freebie.

My ebooks are available via Amazon and Kobo, and the list is growing all the time.

GLADNESS IS INFECTIOUS

Thanks for buying this. You can do me one more favor by leaving a review at the place where you purchased it.

www.ingramcontent.com/pod-product-compliance
Lightning Source LLC
Chambersburg PA
CBHW030454010526
44118CB00011B/934